INDIAN *Spa Cuisine*

ISBN: 81-7436-355-6

Published in India by Roli Books in arrangement with Roli & Janssen BV The Netherlands
M-75 Greater Kailash II (Market), New Delhi 110 048, India Ph: ++91-11-29212782, 29210886.
Fax: ++91-11-29217185. E-mail: roli@vsnl.com Website: rolibooks.com

Editor: Neeta Datta; Design: Arati Subramanyam
Layout: Kumar Raman; Production: Naresh Nigam, Rakesh Shrivastava

Printed and bound in Singapore

FOREWORD Dr K.K. Aggarwal
President, Heart Care Foundation of India

PHOTOGRAPHS Dheeraj Paul

MANJIT SINGH GILL

INDIAN *Spa Cuisine*

Lustre Press
Roli Books

dedication

To my mother,
Sardarni Dalip Kaur,
who taught me the values of life.

acknowledgements

I wish to thank my father for the values that he has imparted to me; my family, friends and well wishers; most of all my wife, Sally, without whose unrelenting support and perseverance to put up with a chef writer's disorderliness, this book would not have been possible.

I would also like to sincerely thank Mr S. S. H. Rehaman, Executive Director, ITC Ltd., whose appreciation of food has forever been an inspiration to explore deeper into the culinary world.

Mr Nakul Anand, Managing Director ITC Hotels Ltd., receives my heartfelt gratitude for being the driving force behind me in the field of culinary creativity, always keeping my plate full with projects to research upon.

contents

FOREWORD

Food has been alluded to as *Brahman* in the *Upanishads* and is considered as one which nourishes our soul. To acquire health and happiness one needs to live a balanced life. Even in the *Bhagavad Gita* Krishna says to Arjuna, 'For the one whose diet and movements are balanced, who does his actions in a proper manner, whose hour of sleeping and waking up is regular, the path of meditation is the destroyer of pain or unhappiness.' The message is relevant even today, validated by modern scientific research and data analysis. The basic principles of food, both choice and cooking, come from traditional knowledge of Ayurveda which says that a healthy diet should be a mixture of six tastes and seven colours. Ayurveda talks about needs of the patient's recipes, which are specific to an individual and his *doshas*.

It gives me immense pleasure to see that Manjit, whom I have known for decades, has incorporated Ayurvedic principles when writing and choosing recipes whether vegetarian or non-vegetarian for this book. He is one person who integrates health with cooking in his day-to-day life. He has been instrumental in teaching and training people about healthy, low calorie, and tasty cooking. I have seen his enthusiasm since the very first Perfect Health Mela organized at the Talkatora Grounds in 1993, where he demonstrated what healthy cooking includes.

This book is a must for all food lovers as it provides an opportunity for the housewives to plan a complete menu and for party lovers to have food choices, which are not only tasty but also attractive to look at. I feel this book will also serve as a substitute for a chef to any dietician or any diet counsellor, as this book of *Indian Health Cuisine* is based on low calorie healthy yet tasty food, which can be easily made from raw materials available locally for people from all religions in the country.

Dr K. K. Aggarwal
President, Heart Care Foundation of India
Senior Consultant, Mool Chand K. R. Hospital
CMD, IJCP Group of Publications
Medical Director, K. L. Chopra Body Mind Institute

INTRODUCTION

My father, Tara Singh an INA freedom fighter, is 93 years old. He is happy and healthy. He takes care of his health by eating healthy. His diet comprises all essential foods, that is, proteins, fats, carbohydrates, and maintains the desirable body weight.

Being healthy involves the entire being—body, mind and spirit. The power to make ourselves healthy lies within us and it would bear results if we are prepared to follow a strict regime. Moderation is the key. The Indian practice of Ayurveda, a science and art of good living, also holds the promise of prolonging and enhancing the quality of life.

We have the power to convert food into poison and also to turn it into nectar. The choice of lifestyle is entirely ours whether it will or will not enhance our mental, emotional, and spiritual growth and ensure good physical health. To achieve this it is important to have a positive outlook. Attitude is the most important factor for good health. By simply regulating dietary habits, it is possible to remain healthy. Meditation improves mental health and makes one spiritually strong, which is an important part of healthy living.

Food has the unique quality of absorbing from its surrounding. It is therefore necessary that the creator must be endowed with hygiene, health, and freshness. The *Gita* says, 'You are what you eat or tell me what you eat and I will tell you who you are.'

Though Ayurveda is popularly regarded as a stream of traditional medicine, it is much more than that. It is the science of life—the word itself signifies that: *Ayur* means life and *Veda* means knowledge. And the goal of Ayurveda is the pursuit of longevity and complete fulfillment.

Ayurveda talks about complex phenomena like ingestion, digestion, absorption, assimilation, and metabolisms of the five basic elements, namely earth, water, fire, air, and ether, in the human body, which again is a complex conglomerate of these elements and is nourished by them through food. Ayurveda lays stress on the taste of food. Taste, which one can experience, is the common man's key to uncovering the highly complex science of nutrition. The experience of palate triggers a chain of chemical reactions that have an effect on all organs of the body, particularly the digestive system.

A well-balanced diet, according to the principles of Ayurveda, should contain rice, green gram, green vegetables, rock salt, barley, milk, ghee, flesh of animals living in dry zones, honey and hygienically collected rain water. These prescribed food items provide the body with the necessary carbohydrates, proteins, fats, minerals, and vitamins.

Ayurveda does not condemn any kind of food, irrespective of the cooking style and taste. All cuisine subscribes to the ayurvedic values in as far as they are balanced. The interpretations of this great culinary epic could be many, but as a mere *sutradhar* (commentator), I have mine and with conviction, I would like to lay down Charaka's ten commandments.

- Eat food that is freshly cooked.
- Food should be tasty and easy to digest.
- Food needs to be eaten in proper quantities, if not too much, not too less either.
- Food and its courses need to work together, not contradict one another.
- Food should be eaten on an empty stomach after the previous meal has been digested.
- Food should be eaten in a congenial atmosphere and with the appropriate equipment and implements.
- Food should not be eaten hurriedly.
- Food should not been eaten too slowly, lest its flavour be lost.
- Food should be eaten with concentrated attention.
- Food should be eaten to suit one's constitution and temperament.

CALORIE CHART

Food	Serving	Calories
Almonds, roasted	1 cup	970.3
Apple, raw	1	81.4
Bean sprouts, raw	1 cup	31.2
Broccoli, raw	1 cup	24.6
Butter, unsalted	1 tbsp	101.8
Cabbage, green, raw	1 cup	21.4
Carrots, raw	1 cup	26.2
Cauliflower, raw	1 cup	24
Cheese, cottage, low-fat	1 cup	163.6
Chicken, boneless, with skin, broiled	4 oz	266.1
Chickpeas, dry, cooked, no fat added	4 oz	755.7
Corn, yellow, cooked, fat added	1 cup	212.1
Cream, half and half	1 cup	315.5
Cucumber, raw	1 cup	25.3
Dates	1 date	22.8
Egg whole, boiled	1 cup	77.2
Eggplant, cooked, fat added	1 cup	252.4
Fish baked / broiled	4 oz	149.5
Fish battered, fried	4 oz	221.3
Flour, white	1 cup	455

Food	Serving	Calories
Flour, wholewheat	1 cup	406.8
Ghee	1 tbsp	12.1
Honey	1 tbsp	64.4
Lemon juice	1 cup	61
Lettuce, raw	1 cup	7.2
Mango	1	134.6
Milk, whole	1 cup	149.9
Mushrooms, raw	1 cup	17.5
Okra, cooked, fat added	1 cup	102.6
Onion, raw	1 cup	41.8
Orange, raw	1 cup	61.6
Popcorn, plain	1 cup	30.6
Potato, cooked, mashed	1	120.5
Radish	1 cup	.3
Rice, white, cooked	1 cup	262.1
Salmon, steamed or poached	4 oz	162.4
Snow pea (pea pod)	1	26.5
Spinach	1 cup	6.6
Squash, cubed	1 cup	51.8
Sweet potato, boiled	1 cup	146.6
Tomato, red	1	25.8
Turnip, raw	1 cup	35.1
Walnuts, shelled	1 cup	642
Yoghurt, plain, non fat	8 oz	126.6

spiced yoghurt

Yoghurt (*dahi*)	$1^1/_4$ cups / 250 gm / 9 oz
Cumin (*jeera*) powder	$^1/_2$ tsp / 1 gm
Red chilli powder	$^1/_4$ tsp
Salt to taste	
Red chilli flakes	2

1. Whisk the yoghurt till smooth. Mix all the spices and salt.
2. Serve garnished with red chilli flakes.

chana roti

Whole Bengal gram flour (*chane ka atta*)	500 gm / 1.1 lb
Salt	$^1/_2$ tsp / 2 gm
Ghee (optional)	

1. Knead whole gram flour with salt and enough water into a smooth dough.
2. Divide the dough equally into 10 equal portions and shape each into a ball. Roll out each ball into 5-6" diameter with a rolling pin.
3. Cook the roti on a hot griddle (*tawa*), when half cooked, turn it to the other side and cook until fully cooked.
4. Apply ghee on the roti (optional) and serve hot.

tomato chutney

Red tomatoes, medium-sized, finely chopped	425 gm / 15 oz
Mustard (*sarson*) oil	1 tsp / 5 ml
Fenugreek seeds (*methi dana*)	1 tsp / 3 gm
Turmeric (*haldi*) powder	$^1/_2$ tsp / 1 gm
Onions, finely chopped	$^3/_4$ cup / 90 gm / 3 oz
Ginger (*adrak*), finely chopped	$1^1/_4$ tbsp / 30 gm / 1 oz
Garlic (*lasan*), finely chopped	$3^3/_4$ tbsp / 45 gm / $1^1/_2$ oz
Green chillies, finely chopped	2
Rock salt	$1^1/_2$ tsp / 3 gm
Cumin (*jeera*) powder	1 tsp / 2 gm
Mint (*pudina*) leaves, chopped	$2^1/_2$ tbsp / 10 gm

1. Heat the mustard oil in a saucepan; sauté the fenugreek seeds.
2. Add turmeric powder, onions, ginger, garlic, and green chillies; sauté till the mixture is light golden.
3. Add the tomatoes, rock salt, and cumin powder; stir and cook for at least 10 minutes or till it becomes like chutney. Add some water if required.
4. Sprinkle mint leaves and mix well. Remove and let it cool.

BASIC PREPARATIONS

mint chutney

Mint (*pudina*) leaves	250 gm / 9 oz
Dry mango, whole (*amchur*)	2
Green chillies	2
Rock salt	2 tsp / 4 gm
Coconut (*nariyal*), grated	1 cup / 100 gm / 3½ oz

1. Soak the dry mango in ½ cup water for 1 hour. When soft, mash it well.
2. Grind mint leaves, green chillies, rock salt, and mashed dry mango to a fine paste.
3. Add coconut and blend again to a smooth paste.

chicken stock

Chicken bones	1 kg / 2.2 lb
Onions, coarsely chopped	1 cup / 120 gm / 4 oz
Carrots (*gajar*), coarsely chopped	60 gm / 2 oz
Celery, coarsely chopped	25 gm
Cloves (*laung*)	6
Bay leaves (*tej patta*)	2
Cinnamon (*dalchini*), 1" stick	1
Green cardamom (*choti elaichi*)	6
Coriander (*dhaniya*) seeds	1 tbsp / 6 gm
Cold water	8 cups / 2 lt / 64 fl oz

1. Rinse the chicken bones and trim of excess fat.
2. Put all the vegetables in a pan. Add the whole spices tied in a muslin cloth. Cover them with chicken bones. Add water and cook on low heat.
3. Slowly bring the stock to simmer and skim the impurities that come on top.
4. Simmer the stock for minimum 45 minutes. Remove and strain through a muslin cloth. Use as required.

tomato salsa

Tomatoes, chopped	100 gm / 3½ oz
Garlic (*lasan*) cloves, minced	2
Onions, chopped	25 gm
Green chillies, chopped, seeds may be removed (optional)	25 gm
Malt vinegar (*sirka*)	2 tbsp / 30 ml / 1 fl oz
Green coriander (*hara dhaniya*), chopped	1 tbsp / 4 gm
Salt to taste	
Olive oil	1 tbsp / 15 ml

1. Simmer the tomatoes in a saucepan with garlic and onion on low heat for 8-10 minutes.
2. Add the green chillies, malt vinegar, and green coriander; simmer for 5 minutes.
3. Add salt and oil, remove and keep aside to cool.

SOUPS, BEVERAGES & SALADS

spinach soup

Spinach (*palak*), chopped	*500 gm / 1.1 lb*
Vegetable oil	*1 tbsp / 15 ml*
Onions, chopped	*1¾ tsp / 10 gm*
Black pepper (*kali mirch*) powder	*½ tsp / 1 gm*
Salt to taste	
Almond (*badaam*) milk (see p. 18)	*4 tbsp / 60 ml / 2 fl oz*

1. Cook the spinach, uncovered, with ½ cup of water for 2-3 minutes. When cool, blend to a smooth purée.
2. Heat the oil in a pan; sauté the onions till light golden in colour.
3. Add the spinach purée and ¼ cup of water. Bring the mixture to the boil and then simmer for 5 minutes.
4. Season to taste with black pepper and salt. Mix in the almond milk. Remove from heat and serve immediately.

pineapple soup

Pineapple (*ananas*), semi-riped, diced	*2 cups*
Water	*3½ cups / 800 ml / 28 fl oz*
Salt and black pepper (*kali mirch*) powder to taste	
Cumin (*jeera*) seeds, crushed	*1 tsp / 2 gm*
Cinnamon (*dalchini*), powdered	*½ tsp / 1 gm*
Honey	*½ tbsp*
Butter	*1 tsp / 5 gm*
Pineapple, sliced for garnishing	

1. Heat the water in a pan and boil the pineapple for 5-7 minutes. Remove from heat and keep aside to cool.
2. Pass the mixture through a soup strainer and keep aside.
3. Season to taste with salt and pepper. Add cumin powder.
4. Reheat the soup and bring to the boil. Stir in the honey and butter.
5. Serve immediately, garnished with pineapple slices.

cucumber & tomato juice

Cucumber (*khira*), cut into strips	*8*
Tomatoes, quartered	*200 gm / 7 oz*
Green coriander (*hara dhaniya*), for garnishing	*a few sprigs*

1. Blend the cucumber and tomatoes together to a liquid consistency. Keep aside a few strips of each for garnishing.
2. Transfer the liquid to a tall glass and serve at room temperature garnished with a slice each of cucumber and tomato and a sprig of green coriander.

almond milk

Almonds (*badaam*)	*½ cup / 60 gm / 2 oz*
Water	*1½ cups / 375 ml / 12 fl oz*
Sugar / Honey / Rock candy (*mishri*) to taste	
Green cardamom (*choti elaichi*) to taste	

1. Soak the almonds overnight. Peel and blend with very little water to make a smooth paste.
2. Add the remaining water and mix well.
3. Add sugar / honey / rock candy to taste. Green cardamom powder can be added for flavour.

pumpkin & ginger juice

Pumpkin (*kaddu*), raw chopped	*1*
Ginger (*adrak*), chopped	*3½ tsp / 20 gm*

1. Blend the pumpkin and ginger with 1 cup of water to a smooth consistency.
2. Transfer the contents into serving glasses and serve immediately.

carrot, beetroot & tomato juice

Carrots (*gajar*), raw, peeled, chopped	*250 gm / 9 oz*
Beetroot (*chukander*), raw, peeled, chopped	*100 gm / 3½ oz*
Tomatoes, chopped	*100 gm / 3½ oz*
Celery, chopped	*2 stalks*
Ginger (*adrak*), chopped	*1¾ tsp / 10 gm*
Water	*2 cups / 500 ml / 16 fl oz*

1. Blend all the ingredients together to a smooth consistency.
2. Transfer the contents into serving glasses and serve immediately garnished with celery stalk.

crunchy salad

Cauliflower (*phool gobhi*), florets	*200-400 gm / 7-14 oz*
Tomatoes, blanched	*100-200 gm / 3½-7 oz*
Spring onions (*hara pyaz*), finely chopped	*2-4*
Green coriander (*hara dhaniya*), chopped	*2½-5 tbsp / 10-20 gm*
Green chillies, finely chopped	*2-4*
Lemon (*nimbu*) juice	*1-2 tbsp / 15-30 ml*
Salt to taste	
Honey	*1-2 tbsp / 15-30 ml*
Cumin (*jeera*) seeds, roasted, powdered	*1-2 tsp / 2-4 gm*
Bengal gram (*chana*), roasted	*¼-½ cup / 50-100 gm / 1¾-3½ oz*

1. Mix all the vegetables in a salad bowl. Refrigerate.
2. Combine lemon juice, salt, honey, and cumin seeds together to make the dressing.
3. Serve the dressing along with the carved vegetables on a serving platter.
4. Garnish with roasted Bengal gram.

apple & walnut salad

Apples (*seb*), cored, chopped into pieces	*4*
Walnuts (*akhrot*), shelled, chopped	*40 gm / 1¼ oz*
Yoghurt (*dahi*), hung for 20 minutes	*¾ cup / 150 gm / 5 oz*
Black cardamom (*badi elaichi*) seeds	*1 tsp / 2 gm*
Cabbage (*bandh gobhi*), shredded	*6 tbsp*
Celery stick, julienned	*3*
Raisins (*kishmish*), halved	*5 tsp*
Salt and black pepper (*kali mirch*) powder to taste	

1. Whisk the yoghurt in a bowl; add the apple, half of the walnuts, and black cardamom seeds.
2. Stir in the remaining ingredients and season to taste with salt and black pepper.
3. Transfer the salad into a serving dish and garnish with the remaining walnuts.

CHICKEN

tandoori chicken with roast onions

Chicken, without skin	*2 (500 gm / 1.1 lb each)*
Onions, large	*4*
Sea salt to taste	
Red chilli powder	*1½ tsp / 3 gm*
Malt vinegar (*sirka*)	*2 tbsp / 30 ml / 1 fl oz*
Yoghurt (*dahi*)	*4 tbsp / 125 gm / 4 oz*
Ginger (*adrak*) paste	*1½ tsp / 10 gm*
Garlic (*lasan*) paste	*1 tbsp / 18 gm*
Lemon (*nimbu*) juice	*2 tbsp / 30 ml / 1 fl oz*
Red chilli powder	*1 tsp / 2 gm*
Garam masala	*1½ tsp / 3 gm*
Turmeric (*haldi*) powder	*1 tsp / 2 gm*

1. With a sharp knife make deep incisions 3 on each breasts and thighs, 2 on each drumsticks.
2. Combine salt, red chilli powder, and malt vinegar together. Rub the mixture over the chicken and in the incisions. Keep aside for 10-15 minutes.
3. Whisk the yoghurt (in case the yoghurt has more moisture, then hang in muslin cloth for 10-15 minutes) in a large bowl. Add the remaining ingredients.
4. Remove the chicken from the first marinade and squeeze the excess moisture gently.
5. Rub the yoghurt marinade all over the chicken and in the deep incisions also. Keep aside for 10-15 minutes.
6. Roast the chicken in a preheated oven at 180°C / 350°F. Place the chicken on the rack with a drip tray under it. Roast for 10-12 minutes. Remove from the oven and separate the legs and breasts. Place again on the rack and roast for 3-4 minutes and remove.
7. Meanwhile, peel the onions without cutting the two ends. Make 6-8 deep cuts without separating and roast along with the chicken until the onions are roasted. Remove.
8. Debone the chicken and serve with the roasted onion. Sprinkle lemon juice if desired.

chicken with fenugreek

1. Sprinkle and rub turmeric powder on the chicken breasts. Keep aside for 5 minutes.
2. Rinse the chicken breasts, pat dry and sprinkle salt.
3. Heat the ghee in a pan; sauté the chicken until almost cooked and light brown on both sides. Remove from the pan and keep aside in a warm place.
4. In the same pan, add ginger and sauté for 10 seconds. Mix in the fenugreek leaves and cook on moderate heat until done, stirring occasionally for 15-20 minutes. Add garam masala; mix. Remove from heat.
5. Transfer the fenugreek leaves to the serving platter and place the chicken breasts over it. Sprinkle dry fenugreek powder and drizzle 1 tsp cream on each. Serve hot with chapatti or tandoori roti.

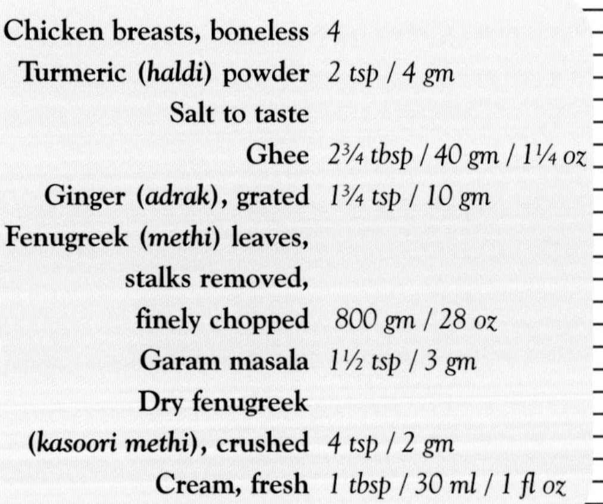

Chicken breasts, boneless	*4*
Turmeric (*haldi*) powder	*2 tsp / 4 gm*
Salt to taste	
Ghee	*2¾ tbsp / 40 gm / 1¼ oz*
Ginger (*adrak*), grated	*1¾ tsp / 10 gm*
Fenugreek (*methi*) leaves, stalks removed, finely chopped	*800 gm / 28 oz*
Garam masala	*1½ tsp / 3 gm*
Dry fenugreek (*kasoori methi*), crushed	*4 tsp / 2 gm*
Cream, fresh	*1 tbsp / 30 ml / 1 fl oz*

chicken & mushrooms in sago roll

Chicken, boneless	*400 gm / 14 oz*
FOR THE MARINADE	
Yoghurt (*dahi*), hung, whisked	*½ cup / 100 gm / 3½ oz*
Turmeric (*haldi*) powder	*1 tsp / 2 gm*
Garam masala	*½ tsp / 1 gm*
Yellow chilli powder	*½ tsp / 1 gm*
Lemon (*nimbu*) juice	*1 tbsp / 15 ml*
Sago (*sabu dana*)	*100 gm / 3½ oz*
Vegetable oil	*1 tbsp / 15 ml*
Onions, finely chopped	*½ cup / 60 gm / 2 oz*
Mushrooms (*gucchi*), sliced	*200 gm / 7 oz*
Salt to taste	
Wholewheat flour (*atta*), kneaded into a semi hard dough	*1 cup / 100 gm / 3½ oz*
Cream	*2 tbsp / 40 ml / 1¼ fl oz*
Eggs, hard-boiled (white only), sliced	2
Sour yoghurt	*2¾ tbsp / 80 gm / 2¾ oz*

1. **For the marinade**, mix all the ingredients together. Rub the marinade into the chicken and keep aside for 30 minutes. Then grill the chicken on a griddle and cut into pieces.
2. Boil some water with salt. Add the sago and bring to the boil, lower heat and simmer for 20-25 minutes until the sago becomes transparent. Remove from heat, drain and rinse under cold water.
3. Heat the oil in a pan; add onions and sauté on low heat until translucent. Increase heat, add mushrooms and cook until the mixture evaporates. Remove from heat and season with salt. Stir in the drained sago, check seasoning and keep aside to cool.
4. Roll out the dough to ⅓" thick rectangle (8" x 6"), cut the edges to make them even and brush the surface of the rectangle with cream leaving a 1" edge on all sides.
5. Place a ¼ of the mushroom mixture in a 2½"-wide strip in the centre of the rectangle. Top with half of the chicken, another layer of mushrooms and sliced egg. Repeat the layering process with the remaining chicken and mushrooms.
6. Fold the edges of the rectangle over the filling to cover completely.
7. Place on a greased baking tray, seam side down and brush the top with cream.
8. Bake in a preheated oven (220°C / 425°C) for 30 minutes or until the dough becomes golden.
9. Remove from the oven, cut into 1½"-wide slices and serve hot, accompanied by sour yoghurt.

See p. 27 (extreme right)

chicken with mango

1. Roast / grill the chicken breasts, one side only.
2. Remove from heat, place on cutting board and keep aside for a few minutes.
3. Remove the skin from the chicken breasts and slice them into 4 equal strips.
4. Evenly coat the strips with stock and keep aside. Arrange the strips on a platter, with a slice of mango between the strips. Decorate with slices of orange.
5. Garnish with honey and serve with mint chutney (see p. 11).

Chicken breasts	*4*
Chicken stock (see p. 11)	*4 tbsp / 60 ml / 2 fl oz*
Mangoes, peeled, sliced	*2*
Orange, peeled, sliced	*2*

chicken with cumin & green gravy

Chicken breasts, boneless	*4*
Green coriander (*hara dhaniya*), washed, chopped	*1 cup / 25 gm*
Mint (*pudina*) leaves, washed, chopped	*5 tbsp / 20 gm*
Green chillies, deseeded, chopped	*4*
Celery, washed, chopped	*30 gm / 1 oz*
Black cumin (*shahi jeera*) seeds	*1 tsp / 2 gm*
Water / Chicken stock (see p. 11)	*2 cups / 500 ml / 16 fl oz*
Barley flour (*jowar ka atta*), roasted	*1 tbsp / 10 gm*
Sea salt to taste	

1. Place the chicken in a pot. Spread green coriander, mint leaves, green chillies, celery, and black cumin seeds evenly over the chicken in the pan.
2. Add water / chicken stock. Bring the mixture to the boil. Reduce heat and simmer for 8-10 minutes or until the chicken is tender.
3. Remove the chicken without removing any of the greens from the pot. Keep the chicken warm.
4. Now blend the remaining mixture to a smooth purée and pour it back into the pan. Bring the purée to the boil on low heat.
5. Dissolve the barley flour in 2 tbsp water and mix with the green gravy. Bring the mixture to the boil and remove from heat. Season with sea salt.
6. Pour the gravy over the chicken and serve hot.

chicken with carrots

Chicken, cut into 1" boneless pieces	*450 gm / 1 lb*
Yoghurt (*dahi*)	*1 cup / 200 gm / 7 oz*
Carrots (*gajar*), peeled, grated	*½ cup*
Green chillies, finely chopped	*2*
Black cumin (*shahi jeera*) seeds	*½ tsp / 1 gm*
Salt to taste	

1. Whisk the yoghurt with ½ cup water; pour into a pan and bring to the boil stirring continuously until reduced to half.
2. Add the carrots and cook for a few minutes. Add chicken, green chillies, black cumin seeds, and salt. Cook until the chicken is tender and the gravy is thick. Remove from heat.
3. Serve hot with poppadums.

shredded chicken with sprouts

Chicken, shredded	*400 gm / 14 oz*
Bean sprouts	*400 gm / 14 oz*
Vegetable oil	*3¼ tbsp / 50 ml / 1¾ fl oz*
Onions, chopped	*½ cup / 60 gm / 2 oz*
Asafoetida (*hing*), soaked in 1 tbsp water	*a pinch*
Turmeric (*haldi*) powder	*½ tsp / 1 gm*
Ginger (*adrak*), grated	*1 tbsp / 12 gm*
Green chillies, chopped	*2*
Coconut (*nariyal*), grated	*1 cup / 100 gm / 3½ oz*

1. Heat the oil in a pan; sauté the onions till golden in colour. Add asafoetida and cook till the moisture evaporates.
2. Add the turmeric powder, chicken, and bean sprouts; mix well.
3. Mix in the ginger and green chillies and cook for 2-3 minutes on high heat. Remove from heat.
4. Serve hot garnished with coconut and accompanied with rice.

FISH

roast salmon with herbs

Salmon, deboned, cut into half lengthwise	*1½ kg / 3.3 lb*
Garlic (*lasan*) clove, halved	*1*
Almond (*badaam*) oil	*3 tbsp / 45 ml / 1½ fl oz*
Green coriander (*hara dhaniya*)	*a few sprigs*
Black cumin (*shahi jeera*) seeds to taste	
Almonds, slivered	*2 tbsp / 30 gm / 1 oz*
Spring onions (white part only), thinly sliced	*3*
Sea salt and black pepper (*kali mirch*) to taste	
Butter	*2 tbsp / 40 gm / 1¼ oz*
Juice of lemon (*nimbu*)	*1*

1. Rub skin of the salmon with cut side of the garlic. Then evenly brush with a film of almond oil.
2. Grease an ovenproof dish. Spread half of the green coriander, some black cumin seeds, and half of the almonds in the centre of the dish. Top with a layer of spring onion and place the salmon over it, skin side up. Brush with almond oil again. Sprinkle the remaining green coriander and black cumin seeds and season with salt and pepper.
3. Heat the oven to 220°C / 425°F. Dot the salmon with butter and sprinkle half of the lemon juice. Roast for 12-15 minutes, until the salmon becomes opaque or roast as per desired.
4. Transfer to a serving dish and keep warm.
5. Heat the remaining butter in a pan; add remaining lemon juice and almonds. Stir-fry for a minute and remove from heat.
6. Pour the butter-almond mixture over the salmon and serve garnished with green coriander.

fish with wheatmeal

Fish fillets (salmon or sole)	*8 / 400 gm / 14 oz*
Salt to taste	
Green chillies, finely chopped	*2*
Milk	*½ cup / 100 ml / 3½ fl oz*
Wheatmeal (*dalia*)	*60 gm / 2 oz*
Vegetable oil	*2 tbsp / 30 ml / 1 fl oz*
Lemon (*nimbu*), cut into wedges for garnishing	
Onion, cut into rings for garnishing	

1. Season the fillets with salt and green chillies. Dip them in milk and coat evenly with wheatmeal.
2. Heat the oil in a non-stick frying pan; gently lower the fillets and fry two at a time. Remove with a slotted spoon and drain the excess oil on absorbent kitchen towels. Repeat till all are fried.
3. Serve hot garnished with lemon and onion rings.

fish marbles with carom seeds

1. Mix the fish, red capsicum, salt, and carom seeds together. Divide the mixture equally into 16 portions. Shape each into marble-sized balls.
2. Heat 1½ cups of water in a pan. Bring to the boil, lower heat and carefully lower the fish balls. Add the ginger and green chillies and simmer until the fish balls are cooked.
3. Remove from heat, place the fish balls on a serving plate along with a few tablespoons of stock. Serve hot garnished with ginger and green chillies.

Fish, sole, minced	*300 gm / 11 oz*
Red capsicum, finely chopped	*20 gm*
Salt to taste	
Carom (*ajwain*) seeds	*1½ tsp / 2½ gm*
Ginger (*adrak*), julienned	*1¾ tsp / 10 gm*
Green chillies, chopped	*4*

pomfret wrapped in papad

1. Marinate the fish with salt, lemon juice, and ginger. Keep aside for 10 minutes.
2. Take a bowl of water, dip each poppadum, one by one and fold around each fillet. Keeping the joint side down.
3. Heat the oil in a non-stick pan; grill the fish, keeping the joint facing the pan, on medium heat until fish is cooked and the poppadum is crisp. Repeat till all are done.
4. Serve hot with salad.

Pomfret fillet	*8 (60 gm / 2 oz)*
Salt to taste	
Lemon (*nimbu*) juice	*1 tbsp / 30 ml / 1 fl oz*
Ginger (*adrak*), grated	*1¾ tsp / 10 gm*
Poppadums (*papad*) with black pepper	*8*
Vegetable oil	*1 tbsp / 15 ml*

salmon steaks with black gram

Salmon steaks	*4 / 120 gm / 4 oz*
Salt to taste	
Juice of lemons (*nimbu*)	*3*
Black gram (*kala chana*), soaked for 4 hours	*150 gm / 5 oz*
Water	*3 cups / 750 ml / 24 fl oz*
Red chilli powder	*1¼ tsp / 2½ gm*
Vegetable oil	*2 tbsp / 30 ml /1 fl oz*
Lettuce leaves, washed	*a few*

1. Mix together the salt and juice of 2 lemons and rub into the steaks. Marinate for 10 minutes.
2. Boil the black gram in a pan. After it comes to the boil, reduce heat and simmer until tender. Add salt and remove from heat. Keep aside ⅓ of the gram mixture for garnishing.
3. Blend the remaining boiled gram into a smooth purée. Add red chilli powder and juice of 1 lemon. Adjust seasoning
4. Heat the oil in a pan, cook the salmon steaks till done.
5. Line a plate with lettuce leaves, place the steaks on the leaves and garnish with the reserved black gram. Serve immediately with black gram sauce on the side.

fish with orange & snow peas

1. Take 1½ cups of water in a flat pan. Add ginger, salt, and crushed black peppercorns. Lower the fish fillets carefully and bring the mixture to the boil. Reducer heat and cook covered for 4-5 minutes or until cooked. Remove the fillets.
2. Boil the stock further till reduced to half.
3. Dissolve the barley flour in 2 tbsp water and add to the stock. Stir continuously till the stock thickens.
4. Place the fillets on a plate, pour the sauce over and serve with orange slices and snow peas.

Salmon fillets	4 (*100 gm / 3½ oz each*)
Ginger (*adrak*), grated	*1 tbsp / 20 gm*
Salt to taste	
Black peppercorns (*sabut kali mirch*), crushed	*½ tsp / 3 gm*
Barley flour (*jowar ka atta*), roasted	*1 tbsp / 10 gm*
Oranges, peeled, sliced	*2*
Snow peas, blanched	*50 gm / 1¾ oz*

VEGETARIAN

stir fried figs

Figs (*anjeer*), fresh, halved	*200 gm / 7 oz*
Vegetable oil	*4 tsp / 20 ml*
Cumin (*jeera*) seeds	*½ tsp / 1 gm*
Asafoetida (*hing*), dissolved in 1 tbsp water	*¼ tsp*
Salt to taste	
Dry red chillies (*sookhi lal mirch*), sliced	*2*

1. Heat the oil in a pan; add the cumin seeds and sauté till it starts spluttering. Add asafoetida and stir until the moisture evaporates completely.
2. Add the figs and cook for 3-4 minutes, stirring continuously. Add the dry red chillies; stir-fry for a minute and serve immediately.

new potatoes with spinach

New potatoes, washed, boiled, peeled	*600 gm / 22 oz*
Vegetable oil	*2 tbsp / 30 ml / 1 fl oz*
Cumin (*jeera*) seeds	*1 tsp / 2 gm*
Ginger (*adrak*), finely chopped	*1¾ tsp / 10 gm*
Salt to taste	
Spinach, washed in running water	*200 gm / 7 oz*

1. Heat the oil in a pan; add the cumin seeds. Sauté until it starts spluttering. Add the potatoes and sauté for a minute.
2. Add ginger and salt; stir-fry for a minute.
3. Add spinach, stir and cover for a minute. Remove cover and stir-fry until the leaves are tender (should not take more than 2-3 minutes). Remove and serve hot.

vegetable idli

Lentil (*masoor dal*)	*1 cup / 100 gm / 3½ oz*
Semolina (*suji*)	*3 cups / 300 gm / 11 oz*
Salt to taste	
Turmeric (*haldi*) powder	*1 tsp / 2 gm*
Carrots (*gajar*), peeled, shredded	*25 gm*
Cabbage (*bandh gobhi*), shredded	*25 gm*
Green peas (*hara matar*), shelled	*25 gm*

1. Soak the lentil and semolina for 6 hours and 1 hour respectively.
2. Wash the lentil and semolina, drain and grind together to a thick paste.
3. Add salt to taste and turmeric powder.
4. Grease the *idli* moulds, place the shredded vegetables in the moulds and pour the batter on top. Steam in the *idli* cooker for 7-10 minutes. Repeat till all the batter is used up.
5. Serve hot with tomato chutney (see p. 10).

capsicum stuffed with idli

Capsicum (*Shimla mirch*)	4
Idli (see p. 58)	4
FOR THE TEMPERING:	
Vegetable oil	*4 tsp / 20 ml*
Mustard seeds (*rai*)	*1 tsp / 3 gm*
Turmeric (*haldi*) powder	*1 tsp / 2 gm*
Curry leaves (*kadhi patta*)	8
Green chilli, finely chopped	*1*

1. Slice the stalks of the capsicum and deseed. Blanch them in boiling water for 5 minutes. Drain and keep aside.
2. **For the stuffing**, cool and cut the *idli* into small pieces.
3. **For the tempering**, heat the oil in a pan; sauté the mustard seeds till it starts spluttering. Add turmeric powder, curry leaves, and green chilli; cook for a minute. Pour the tempering over the *idli*.
4. Stuff the capsicum with the tempered *idli*. Transfer to a greased ovenproof dish and bake in a preheated oven (160°C / 325°F) for 10-12 minutes.
5. Remove and serve immediately with tomato chutney (see p. 10).

See p. 53 (extreme right)

stuffed courgettes

Courgettes (*lauki*), washed, stems removed, scraped	*2 / 450 gm / 16 oz*
Ginger (*adrak*) paste	*3 tbsp / 54 gm / 1¾ oz*
Garlic (*lasan*) paste	*1¾ tsp / 10 gm*
Lemon (*nimbu*) juice	*4 tbsp / 60 ml / 2 fl oz*
Yellow chilli powder	*1 tsp / 2 gm*
Salt to taste	
Vegetable oil	*3 tbsp / 45 ml / 1½ fl oz*
FOR THE FILLING:	
Cottage cheese (*paneer*), diced	*300 gm / 11 oz*
Carrots (*gajar*), diced	*50 gm / 1¾ oz*
Capsicum (*Shimla mirch*), diced	*30 gm / 1 oz*
Ginger, diced	*½ tbsp / 12 gm*
Green coriander (*hara dhaniya*), finely chopped	*1 tbsp / 4 gm*
Garam masala	*1 tsp / 2 gm*
Salt	*1 tsp / 4 gm*

1. Core the length of each courgette ½ cm walls to form tubes. Finely chop the marrow meat.
2. Mix ginger paste, garlic paste, lemon juice, yellow chilli powder, and salt together. Rub this mixture inside and outside the bottle gourd.
3. Heat the oil in a pan; add the marrow meat and stir until cooked.
4. **For the filling**, mix the cottage cheese, carrots, capsicum, ginger, green coriander, garam masala, and salt with the cooked marrow meat. Divide the mixture into 2 equal portions.
5. Stuff each marrow with a portion of the stuffing. Seal each end with foil. Brush some oil on the marrow.
6. Bake in a preheated oven at 180°C / 350°F for 20-25 minutes.
7. Remove and keep aside to cool for 10 minutes. Slice and serve with tomato chutney and chana roti (see p. 10).

grilled vegetables with yoghurt sauce

Bell peppers, cut into halves	*50 gm / 1¾ oz*
Carrots (*gajar*), sliced	*80 gm / 2¾ oz*
Onions, quartered	*50 gm / 1¾ oz*
Cabbage (*bandh gobhi*) leaves, separated	*100 gm / 3½ oz*
FOR THE SAUCE:	
Vegetable oil	*4 tsp / 20 ml*
Garlic (*lasan*), finely chopped	*1¾ tsp / 10 gm*
Yoghurt (*dahi*)	*½ cup / 100 gm / 3½ oz*
Curry powder	*2½ tsp / 5 gm*
Salt to taste	

1. Grill all the vegetables in a non-stick pan and keep aside.
2. **For the sauce**, heat the oil in a pan; add the garlic and yoghurt; sauté for 2-3 minutes.
3. Stir in the curry powder and salt; remove from heat.
4. Arrange the vegetables on a plate and pour the sauce on top.

aubergine with vegetables & honey

Aubergine (*baingan*), round, cut into ½"-thick slices	*1*
Carrots (*gajar*), peeled, chopped into 1" pieces	*100 gm / 3½ oz*
Turnips (*shalgam*), peeled, chopped into 1" pieces	*100 gm / 3½ oz*
Pumpkin (*kaddu*)	*100 gm / 3½ oz*
Courgette (*lauki*), peeled, chopped into 1" pieces	*100 gm / 3½ oz*
French beans, strings removed, chopped into 1" pieces	*100 gm / 3½ oz*
Vegetable oil	*1 tbsp / 15 ml*
Cumin (*jeera*) seeds	*1 tsp / 2 gm*
Salt to taste	
Honey	*4 tbsp / 60 ml / 2 fl oz*

1. Soak the aubergine in water and keep aside.
2. Boil the vegetables in individual lots till almost done.
3. Drain the aubergine, sprinkle some salt and keep aside.
4. Heat the oil in a pan; add cumin seeds and sauté till it starts spluttering. Add the vegetables and toss for a few minutes. Season to taste with salt and remove from heat.
5. Place one portion of the vegetables on each aubergine slice, drizzle 1 tsp honey on top and serve.

semiya upma

Vermicelli (*semiya*)	*250 gm / 9 oz*
Vegetable oil	*1¾ tbsp / 25 ml*
Bengal gram (*chana dal*)	*1 tbsp / 25 gm*
Cumin (*jeera*) seeds	*a pinch*
Turmeric (*haldi*) powder	*½ tsp / 1 gm*
Green peas (*hara matar*), boiled	*25 gm*
Salt to taste	

1. Heat the oil in a thick-bottomed pan; add the Bengal gram and cumin seeds. Sauté till the Bengal gram changes colour to golden brown and the cumin seeds start spluttering.
2. Add vermicelli and sauté further for a few seconds. Add turmeric powder and enough water to cover. Boil continuously for 1 minute.
3. Add green peas and salt, lower heat and cook covered for 5 minutes.
4. Serve hot.

See p. 52 (extreme left)

grilled mushrooms with tomato salsa

1. Heat 1 tbsp oil in a pan; add the mushrooms and cook until the moisture evaporates. Remove and keep aside to cool.
2. When cool, blend the mushrooms to a coarse mixture.
3. Heat the remaining oil in a thick-bottomed pan; add the barley flour and sauté for a minute. Pour in the milk and bring to the boil. Lower heat and simmer, stirring continuously, until the mixture reaches a thick sauce-like consistency.
4. Add mushroom mixture and green coriander; mix well. Check seasoning and keep aside to cool.
5. Divide the mixture equally into small portions. Shape each like a mushroom and grill on a hot plate or on a non-stick pan till light golden. Repeat till all are done. Serve with tomato salsa (see p. 11).

Mushrooms (*gucchi*), washed, chopped	*500 gm / 1.1 lb*
Vegetable oil	*3 tbsp / 45 ml / 1½ fl oz*
Barley flour (*jowar ka atta*), roasted	*60 gm / 2 oz*
Milk	*5 tbsp / 75 ml / 2½ fl oz*
Green coriander (*hara dhaniya*), finely chopped	*2½ tbsp / 10 gm*
Salt to taste	
Black pepper (*kali mirch*), freshly crushed	*1 tsp / 2 gm*

mushrooms with fenugreek

Mushrooms (*gucchi*), washed in running water	*400 gm / 14 oz*
Fenugreek (*methi*) leaves, washed	*800 gm / 28 oz*
Vegetable oil	*2¾ tbsp / 40 ml*
Ginger (*adrak*), grated	*1¾ tsp / 10 gm*
Salt to taste	
Black peppercorns (*sabut kali mirch*), freshly crushed	*½ tsp / 3 gm*
Garam masala	*1 tsp / 2 gm*

1. Boil ½ cup of water with a little salt and 1 tbsp lemon juice. Add the mushrooms, stir and cook covered for 2 minutes. Remove from heat and keep covered. When the mixture cools down a bit remove the mushrooms and cut into quarters. Reserve the stock and use in soups.
2. Remove the hard stalks and finely chop the fenugreek leaves.
3. Heat 2 tbsp oil in a pan; add ginger and stir. Add fenugreek and cook on medium heat, stirring occasionally. Stir in the salt, black pepper, and garam masala; cook for 30 seconds more. Remove.
4. Heat the remaining oil in a pan; toss the mushrooms for 30-45 seconds. Remove and sprinkle some dry fenugreek leaves.
5. Serve the mushrooms with fenugreek.

spinach and tomato shashlik

Spinach (*palak*)	*600 gm / 22 oz*
Tomatoes, deseeded, cut into 1" squares	*400 gm / 14 oz*
Capsicum (*Shimla mirch*), deseeded, cut into 1" squares	*50 gm / 1¾ oz*
Vegetable oil	*2 tsp / 10 ml*
Cumin (*jeera*) seeds	*1 tsp / 2 gm*
Onions, finely chopped	*½ cup / 60 gm / 2 oz*
Ginger (*adrak*), grated	*1¾ tsp / 10 gm*
Cottage cheese (*paneer*), grated	*50 gm / 1¾ oz*
Salt to taste	
Tomato purée	*¼ cup / 50 ml / 1¾ fl oz*
Honey	*1 tbsp / 15 ml*

1. Wash the spinach leaves in running water for 2-3 minutes. Drain well.
2. Blanch in boiling water for 2 minutes. Remove and keep in chilled water.
3. Heat the oil in a pan; add the cumin seeds and sauté until it starts spluttering. Add the onions and sauté until translucent. Stir in the ginger and cottage cheese; sauté until the moisture evaporates. Remove and keep aside to cool. Add salt and mix well.
4. Spread the spinach leaves on a flat surface, put the cottage cheese mixture in the centre and fold like parcels. Keep aside.
5. Skewer alternately, squares of capsicum, tomatoes, and spinach parcels.
6. Make a marinade by mixing tomato purée and honey together. Rub the marinade over the shashlik and grill on a hot plate or in a non-stick pan until lightly charred from all sides. Serve immediately with spiced yoghurt (see p. 10).

broccoli in cottage cheese sauce

Broccoli, medium-sized florets	*500 gm / 1.1 lb*
Milk	*1 cup / 200 ml / 7 fl oz*
Cottage cheese (*paneer*), grated	*80 gm / 2¾ oz*
Yellow chilli powder	*1 tsp / 2 gm*
Nutmeg (*jaiphal*), grated or powdered	*1 tsp / 3 gm*
Salt to taste	
Almonds (*badaam*), roasted, slivered	*1 tbsp / 15 gm*

1. Heat the milk in a pan and bring to the boil. Reduce heat and stir in the cottage cheese. Cook until it reaches a sauce-like consistency.
2. Add yellow chilli powder, nutmeg, and salt. Stir well and remove from heat.
3. In a separate pan, boil some water. Add broccoli and a little salt. Cook for 4-5 minutes, remove from heat and drain.
4. Arrange the broccoli on a platter, pour the prepared cottage cheese sauce on top, garnish with almonds and serve immediately.

cottage cheese with French beans

1. Heat the oil in a pan; add the mustard seeds and sauté till it starts spluttering. Add French beans and toss on low heat until tender.
2. Add the tomatoes and salt, cook for a few minutes, stirring occasionally. Remove from heat and keep aside.
3. Heat a non-stick pan, brush with oil and place the cottage cheese steaks on it. Grill evenly on both sides, remove from heat and keep aside.
4. Place a layer of French beans on a serving platter, top with cottage cheese steaks and serve immediately with a dash of lemon juice.

Cottage cheese (*paneer*) steaks	*80 gm / 2¾ oz*
French beans, chopped	*250 gm / 9 oz*
Vegetable oil	*4 tsp / 20 ml*
Mustard seeds (*rai*)	*1 tsp / 3 gm*
Tomatoes, blanched, deseeded, chopped	*100 gm / 3½ oz*
Salt to taste	
Lemon (*nimbu*) juice	*1 tbsp / 15 ml*

stuffed vine leaves with tomato chutney

Vine leaves, washed	*18*
Unpolished rice, washed, soaked for 1 hour	*¼ cup / 50 gm / 1¾ oz*
Olive oil	*5 tsp / 25 ml*
Dill (*sooya*), fresh, finely chopped	*5 gm*
Lemon (*nimbu*) juice	*1 tbsp / 15 ml*
Black pepper (*kali mirch*), freshly crushed	*¼ tsp*
Salt to taste	
Raisins (*kishmish*)	*18*

1. Boil the rice until almost done; drain in a sieve and set aside.
2. Heat 2 tsp oil in a pan on medium heat; add dill, lemon juice, black pepper, and salt. Cook for 2-3 minutes, stirring constantly. Remove from heat and mix in the raisins and rice.
3. Bring 3 cups of water to the boil in a pan on high heat. Add the vine leaves and bring to the boil; remove the pan from the heat. Let the leaves soak in the hot water for 3-4 minutes, then pour off the water and dip the leaves in cold water to cool them quickly. Gently separate the leaves and spread them on paper or kitchen towel to remove excess water.
4. Place the leaves dull side up and put 1 tbsp of rice mixture on the centre of a leaf. Turn up the stem end and then, one at a time fold over each of the sides to enclose the stuffing completely. Starting again at the stem end, roll the leaf gently but firmly into a compact cylinder. Repeat with other leaves.
5. Layer the bottom of a casserole with 6 leaves. Arrange the stuffed leaves, side by side, seam side down. Sprinkle 3 tsp olive oil and ½ cup of cold water. Bring to the boil, lower heat and simmer, tightly covered, for 30-35 minutes. Then uncover and cool to room temperature.
6. Arrange the stuffed leaves on tomato chutney (see p. 10).

ACCOMPANIMENTS

corn & cinnamon rice

Cooked Basmati rice	*200 gm / 7 oz*
Corn (*bhutta*), boiled	*100 gm / 3½ oz*
Vegetable oil	*4 tsp / 20 ml*
Cinnamon (*dalchini*) powder	*1 tsp / 2 gm*
Popcorn	*20 gm*
Salt to taste	

1. Heat the oil in a pan; add the corn and toss. Add cinnamon powder and mix well. Add the rice and toss well. Season with salt.
2. Serve garnished with popcorn.

rice with potatoes

Cooked rice	*400 gm / 14 oz*
Potatoes, diced	*200 gm / 7 oz*
Vegetable oil	*2¾ tbsp / 40 ml / 1¼ fl oz*
Mustard seeds (*rai*)	*¼ tsp*
Cumin (*jeera*) seeds	*¼ tsp*
Asafoetida (*hing*)	*¼ tsp*
Turmeric (*haldi*) powder	*¼ tsp*
Poppadums (*papad*)	*2*
Green coriander (*hara dhaniya*), chopped	*2½ tbsp / 10 gm*

1. Heat the oil in a pan; add the mustard seeds, cumin seeds, and asafoetida. When they start spluttering, add turmeric powder and stir.
2. Add the potatoes and sauté till cooked. Add the rice and mix well. Remove from heat.
3. Cut the poppadums into strips and roast. Serve the potato rice garnished with roasted poppadums and green coriander.

barley cakes

Barley (*jowar*), soaked, boiled	*50 gm / 1¾ oz*
Potatoes, mashed	*400 gm / 14 oz*
Vegetable oil	*1 tbsp / 15 ml*
Cumin (*jeera*) seeds	*1 tsp / 2 gm*
Onions, finely chopped	*50 gm / 1¾ oz*
Garlic (*lasan*), finely chopped	*1¾ tsp / 10 gm*
Spinach (*palak*), blanched, chopped	*200 gm / 7 oz*
Salt to taste	

1. Heat the oil in a pan on medium heat; add cumin seeds and sauté until it starts spluttering. Add onions and garlic and sauté until light golden. Add spinach and sauté until the moisture evaporates. Remove from heat and keep aside to cool.
2. Add the boiled barley, mashed potatoes and salt; mix well. Divide the mixture equally and shape into little cakes. Grill the cakes in a non-stick pan on both sides till golden.

pickled onions

Onions, small, cut the top and bottom	*400 gm / 14 oz*
White vinegar (*sirka*)	*2½ tbsp / 40 ml / 1¼ fl oz*
Castor sugar	*40 gm / 1¼ oz*
Olive oil	*3 tbsp / 45 ml / 1½ fl oz*
Lemon (*nimbu*) juice	*2 tbsp / 30 ml / 1 fl oz*
Coriander (*dhaniya*) seeds	*1 tsp / 2 gm*
Bay leaf (*tej patta*)	*1*
Salt to taste	
Black peppercorns (*sabut kali mirch*), crushed	*½ tsp / 3 gm*
Tomatoes, blanched, finely chopped	*60 gm / 2 oz*
Basil (*tulsi*)	*4 sprigs*

1. Bring 4 cups / 1 lt of water to the boil. Blanch the onions in the water for a minute. Drain and cool slightly before peeling the onions.
2. Combine vinegar, castor sugar, olive oil, lemon juice, coriander seeds, bay leaf, salt, black pepper, tomatoes, and 620 ml water together in a large pot. Add the onions, bring to the boil and simmer for 20 minutes or until the mixture has been reduced to ¾th. Remove the bay leaf. Cool and chill for a few hours.
3. Serve onion pickle with basil sprig on top.

DESSERTS

melon cups

Melons, small	6
Mixed fruits (strawberries, raspberries, black currants, cherries, small chunks of peach, orange)	*450 gm / 16 oz*
Lemon (*nimbu*) juice	*a few drops*
Sugar to taste	
Mint (*pudina*)	*small sprigs*

1. Slice the tops of the melons and keep aside. Scoop out most of the flesh from the centre with a pointed spoon and discard the seeds. Put the flesh in a bowl with any juice that is produced. Add a few mint leaves.
2. Add the mixed fruits. Mix in the lemon juice and sugar as per taste. Fill the melon cups with this mixture and chill till ready to serve.
3. Serve garnished with a mint sprig and replace the lid at an angle.

apple kheer

Milk	*2¼ cups / 450 ml / 15 fl oz*
Apples (*seb*), grated with skin	*200 gm / 7 oz*
Sago (*sabu dana*)	*50 gm / 1¾ oz*
Cinnamon (*dalchini*) powder	*a pinch*
Green cardamom (*choti elaichi*) powder	*¼ tsp*
Honey	*4 tbsp / 60 ml / 2 fl oz*

1. Soak the sago in water for 30 minutes.
2. Bring the milk to the boil. Add the drained sago and cook for 5-6 minutes.
3. Add the apple, stir and simmer for 5-6 minutes or until it reaches a semi-thick consistency.
4. Add cinnamon powder and green cardamom powder; stir.
5. Remove from heat and keep aside to cool. Serve chilled drizzled with honey.

egg white dumplings with semolina sauce

Egg whites	*4*
Sugar	*100 gm / 3½ oz*
Milk	*2½ cups / 500 ml / 16 fl oz*
Green cardamom (*choti elaichi*) powder	*1 tsp / 2 gm*
Semolina (*suji*)	*2½ tbsp / 25 gm*
Mint (*pudina*)	*4 sprigs*

1. Take the egg whites in a clean bowl and whisk at moderate speed or with an electric egg beater till white like snow. Add 80 gm / 2¾ oz sugar and whisk simultaneously until stiff peaks form.
2. Heat 1¼ cups / 250 ml milk in a pan; add green cardamom powder and bring to the boil. Reduce heat and simmer.
3. Scoop out 8 dumplings of egg white with a tablespoon and poach in the simmering milk until they firm up. Remove carefully and keep aside.
4. Stir-fry the semolina until a pleasing smell emanates. Add the remaining milk and cook until thick. Add the remaining sugar; mix well and remove.
5. Pour the sauce on a plate and arrange the egg white dumplings with mint sprigs.

See p. 87 (extreme right)

strawberry yoghurt

1. Remove and discard the green from the top of the strawberries.
2. Hang the yoghurt in a muslin cloth for 20 minutes. Remove from the cloth and blend with strawberries (keep aside a few for garnishing) and green peppercorns. Add sugar and blend well.
3. Serve garnished with strawberries.

See p. 86 (second from left)

Strawberries, fresh	*100 gm / 3½ oz*
Yoghurt (*dahi*)	*1 cup / 200 gm / 7 oz*
Green peppercorns, crushed	*½ tsp*
Low calorie sugar to taste	

popcorn chikki with yoghurt & fruits

1. Hang the yoghurt in a muslin cloth for 30 minutes in the refrigerator.
2. Meanwhile, cut the fruits in fancy shapes or which ever way you like.
3. Heat the jaggery in a pan until it melts. Add popcorn and mix well so that the popcorn is well coated. Then spread them on an oiled surface and crush with a rolling pin until 1 cm thick. Cut into 8 discs.
4. Remove the yoghurt and whisk well.
5. Arrange one disc on a serving plate, pour the yoghurt on the side with the fruits arranged neatly. Place another disc on the yoghurt and serve.

Popcorn, plain	*120 gm / 4 oz*
Yoghurt (*dahi*)	*2½ cups / 500 gm / 16 fl oz*
Fruits (apples, cherries, oranges)	
Jaggery (*gur*)	*¾ cup / 150 gm / 5 oz*
Mint (*pudina*)	*4 sprigs*

index

soups, beverages & salads

chicken

fish

vegetarian

accompaniments

desserts

AF543492